Organized for Success!

Organized for Success!

95 Tips for Taking Control of Your Time, Your Space—and Your Life

Nanci McGraw

SkillPath Publications
Mission, KS

Editor: Kelly Scanlon

Page Layout and Design: Rod Hankins, Mary Dempsey

Cover Design: Rod Hankins

Cover Illustration: Steve Shamburger

Library of Congress Catalog Card Number: 95-74679

ISBN: 978-1-878542-79-3

Printed in the United States of America

Contents

CONTENTS

Lessons About Life

(Don't skip over this page.)

- "One of these days…" is none of these days, unless you make it happen.

- Whatever state things are in, you better not get used to it; things will change soon.

- In life, everything is in a constant state of change, sometimes fast and sometimes slow.

- Eventually something will need moving, fixing, dusting or sorting.

- Having a system for moving from one change to another helps the transition process. Getting organized means developing such a system.

- Getting organized is not something you do just once. It's an ongoing process. Not only must you maintain your system, you must be prepared to change it as your circumstances and situation change. Often, the organizational system that handles the change must change.

- Since you're not in control of all changes, you can at least be more comfortable when you control your response to the change. Without a system in place, you'll find yourself reacting to the change—letting it control you.

So, getting organized means TAKING CONTROL of systems that help you accommodate and even embrace the change. When you can do that, you can maintain relationships with the people and stay focused on the projects that have priority in your life.

That's what this book is all about.

Acknowledgments

My personal motto for life and everything I do is:

"Add Zip to the Trip!"

For this book project and life in general, I readily acknowledge many people who assist in making the motto happen.

Enthusiastic thanks to:

- Mom and Dad Jones, who set me on life's trip and even tolerate and act like they enjoy my zip.

- Barbara, Marilyn and Brian and their families, my siblings on the trip. They add their own brand of zip.

- Bob, my husband and chosen team member for the trip. He encourages me and even says he loves my zip.

- Darrin, Heather and Gavin, my special children. They always add zip of their own to everybody's trip.

ACKNOWLEDGMENTS

- Zippy friends, professional colleagues and acquaintances too numerous to list, who inspire me to make sure my trip is taking me where I want to go.

- All who cross my path in personal and professional circles, encouraging me in my ongoing goal of getting organized; that is, in TAKING CONTROL of the trip.

Introduction

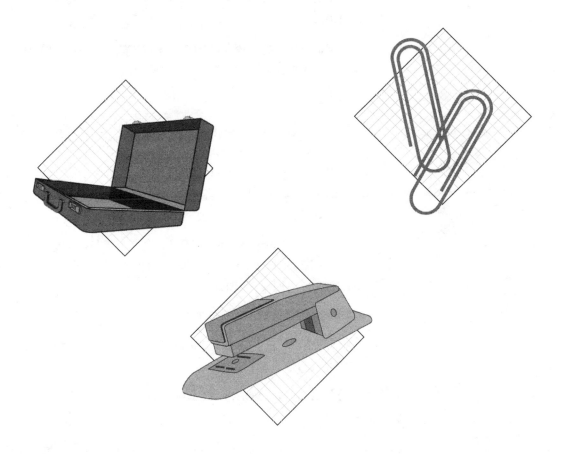

INTRODUCTION

Who Needs This Book?

Three types of people need this book:

1. People who are so disorganized they don't have time for books

2. People who are organized enough to know they can never be organized enough

3. You!

Organized for Success! can help you do something you've been meaning to do for a long time: Get organized. In *Organized for Success!,* you'll discover time-proven tips for organizing your work space, your time—and your life.

More specifically, you'll learn ways for dealing with each of the following situations so you can work more efficiently and productively:

- How to cope with clutter

- How the layout of your work space affects your work habits

- How your work style affects your productivity

- How to manage back-breaking loads of reading material

- How to set up a filing system that not only organizes your important documents—but also allows you to find them fast

- How to use your computer to speed up routine tasks—and tricks for keeping your electronic files organized

You'll also find encouragement and specific ideas for maximizing traditional To Do lists and organizers, and even a use you may not have thought of for that faithful old briefcase.

How to Get the Most Out of This Book

Organized for Success! is concise and to the point. Every chapter contains Taking Control Tips that take only a few minutes to read, but they can save you hours of time later. Each chapter is self-contained so you can read the book from cover to cover or skip directly to the chapter that addresses your most pressing TAKING CONTROL need.

"Every noble work is at first impossible."
—Thomas Carlyle

INTRODUCTION

Do whatever works to help you get more organized.

As you read the book, keep a highlighter in hand to mark the Taking Control Tips that would benefit you, do the exercises and then schedule time over the next week to ten days to carry out the suggestions in some of the Taking Control Tips you highlighted. Actually scheduling the time will commit you to taking action.

Keep the book in your work area and set a goal to come back again and again for more ideas to implement.

Organization (the theory) really begins in your head and then slides down to your heart (inspiration) and then moves to your hands and body (perspiration). So, you must *know* what it takes to get organized, make the *commitment* to doing it and then do it. Only then will you be in CONTROL—not only of your time and space, but of your life as well.

Taking Control of Your Time

Getting From Here to There

SECTION • ONE

Think about what it would mean to your life and career to know that:

- Your priorities are in place.

- Your work area encourages you to work.

- You're completing your work in a timely way.

- Your life has a healthy balance.

- You're able to concentrate on the task at hand.

- You're using energies creatively and productively.

What would it mean?

It means you are getting and staying organized so you can be on top of things. It means your days of simply reacting to events and circumstances are over because you have a system in place that anticipates them. It means you are TAKING CONTROL.

"Organizing is what you do before you do something, so that when you do it, it's not all mixed up."

—Christopher Robin, in *Winnie the Pooh* by A.A. Milne

Getting From Here to There

You *Can* Get There From Here

There is that place where you feel you are taking control of your life and your space.

Here is whenever you feel things and events are taking control of you.

There is where you have:

- Less clutter.
- Less stress.
- Less to fix, clean and dust.
- Less to remember.

Some people are constantly looking for more stuff, status symbols or more things to prove they have "arrived." Try a different kind of *more:*

- More order
- More enjoyment
- More peace and tranquillity
- More purposeful accomplishment

So how do you get "there" from "here"?

Read on to find out.

"I expect to spend the rest of my life in the future, so I want to be reasonably sure of what kind of future it's going to be."
—Charles Kettering

SECTION • ONE

<u>TAKING CONTROL TIP #1</u>

You must first analyze your current situation
to pinpoint the areas of your life where you're
wasting or inefficiently using your time, energy
and resources.

Take the quiz that follows to help you identify these
troublespots. Then, read the Taking Control Tips
scattered throughout this book for ideas for taking
control of those troublesome areas so you can
focus on what matters most to you—your priorities.

*"The one lesson
I have learned in
life is that there is
no substitute for
paying attention."*

—Diane Sawyer

CHAPTER • ONE

Getting From Here to There

Take a "quiz"-zical look at the possible areas of disorganization in your life. Use the following notation:

A = Always

B = Most of the time

C = Often

D = Once in a while

Exercise One

HOW FAR OUT OF CONTROL IS MY LIFE AND MY SPACE?

1. I am swamped with paperwork. _____

2. I let magazines pile up without reading them. _____

3. I clip articles but don't get around to reading them. _____

4. My desk is covered with piles of papers, files and books. _____

5. My computer files aren't backed up. _____

6. My computer files are disorganized. _____

7. My CDs and DVDs are in a hodgepodge. _____

8. I often spend more than thirty seconds looking for items in or on my desk. _____

9. My work tools are in disarray. _____

10. More paper comes into my office
    than goes out. _____

11. I find it difficult to throw things away. _____

12. I'm often late and I sometimes
    miss appointments. _____

13. I misplace small pieces of paper
    and sticky notes. _____

14. People put items on my chair or
    computer so I'll be sure to see them. _____

15. My In box is always full. _____

16. I work at another place because
    my desk is so messy. _____

17. I don't use my computer to get
    organized or to automate routine jobs. _____

18. I struggle with conflicting deadlines
    and demands on my time. _____

19. I use filing cabinets to hide desk
    items when visitors come. _____

Getting From Here to There

20. I feel discouraged or frustrated
    by my work environment. _____

21. I don't know which are my
    real priorities. _____

22. I start one task and then get distracted
    and move to another one. _____

23. People leave messages for me here
    and there. _____

24. People can't find items that I file
    or put away. _____

25. I dread starting a new project
    because I have so many loose
    ends to tie up on others. _____

"We think in generalities, but we live in detail."

—Alfred North
Whitehead

SECTION • ONE

In the appropriate spaces below, write the number of times you responded with each letter.

A _____ B _____ C _____ D _____

Now take a look at which letter(s) you chose most often. The bottom line is this:

- **Cs and Ds aren't real problems.** It's a fact of life that you'll occasionally be unprepared or disorganized. No one's perfect.

- **Your As and Bs are your real problem areas.** These are the areas where you find yourself in trouble always or most of the time. A preponderance of As and Bs will tell you much about the energy and commitment you'll need for getting organized and TAKING CONTROL, how far you must travel to reach "there" from "here."

*"A problem
well defined is
half solved."*

—Anonymous

14

Finding Your Focus

Taking Control of Your Time

Finding your focus is an important step in TAKING CONTROL of your time and space.

Getting focused in order to take control is a three-step process that involves:

- Identifying your values.
- Writing a mission statement.
- Setting your priorities.

"Fantasies are more than substitutes for unpleasant reality; they are also dress rehearsals, plans. All acts performed in the world begin in the imagination."

—Barbara G. Harrison

Finding Your Focus

Identifying Your Values

TAKING CONTROL TIP #2

Identify your values.

Your values are the ideas, concepts, goals, people and environmental supports you feel are vital to creating the life you want to live. Your values direct your life and give it quality and meaning.

Complete Exercise #2 to get a handle on what your values are.

"Since I was twenty-four … there never was any vagueness in my plans or ideas as to what God's work was for me."
—Florence Nightingale

Exercise Two

IDENTIFYING MY VALUES

The grid below lists several often-cited values. Circle the ones you feel are vital to you. Add any others that apply specifically to you.

Freedom/Autonomy	Intellectual Growth
Companionship	Respect
Security	Adventure/Excitement
Financial Rewards	Peace/Tranquility
Worship	Camaraderie
Accuracy	Integrity

Finding Your Focus

Personal Expression	Feeling of Accomplishment
Order	Comfort
Recognition	Power
Safety	Creativity
Privacy	Proper Work Space
Entertainment	Other

"The song I came to sing remains unsung. I have spent my life stringing and unstringing my instrument."

—Rabindranath Tagore

Creating a Values Pyramid

Completing Exercise #2 helped you identify your general values. Next, you must order them so you know which ones are most important.

TAKING CONTROL TIP #3

Create a values pyramid.

A values pyramid will give you a graphical representation of how your values rank against each other. Your most important values form the **base** of your pyramid. They are the foundation upon which all your other values are based.

"Try not to become a person of success, but rather to become a person of value."
—Albert Einstein

Finding Your Focus

Here's an example of a values pyramid created from some of the values listed in Exercise #2.

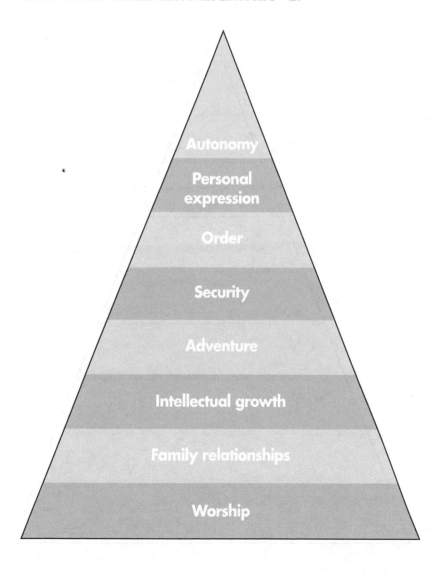

Autonomy

Personal expression

Order

Security

Adventure

Intellectual growth

Family relationships

Worship

"When what you do is in congruity with what you believe, and what you believe is the highest of truths, you achieve the most gratifying form of personal productivity and experience the most satisfying form of self-esteem."

—Charles R. Hobbs, *Time Power*

Taking Control of Your Time

Exercise Three

CREATING A VALUES PYRAMID

Build your values pyramid from the *bottom up.*
Your most important values form the base.

"It's never too late to be what you might have been."
—George Eliot

Finding Your Focus

TAKING CONTROL TIP #4

Be prepared to redo your values pyramid as your life changes.

Because situations and circumstances change, periodically redo your values pyramid to reflect your current situation. Do this without looking at your previous pyramid.

"The heavens themselves, the planets, and this center, observe degree, priority, and place."

—William Shakespeare

The Importance of Mission Statements

TAKING CONTROL TIP #5

Write your very own mission statement.

> *"He turns not back who is bound to a star."*
>
> —Leonardo da Vinci

Now that you have searched your soul and come up with your values, the next step is to make them concrete by writing a mission statement.

Corporations, religious groups, organizations, families and individuals can have mission statements. A mission statement is generally twenty-five words or less and is written in formal language that broadly describes the vision, commitment, focus and level of excellence of the person or organization that writes it. It describes *what* you would like to achieve, but not how you plan to do it. It is a sharing of the vision, not the action plan. It is the setting of a goal to which you aspire, not the steps you'll take to achieve the goal.

Finding Your Focus

Here are some sample mission statements:

- *The purpose of Worldwide Toys is to create and manufacture unique, high-quality, entertaining, educational and safe toys for kids of all ages.*

- *The mission of Silver City Spas is to profitably provide a relaxing and inspiring environment where both patrons and employees focus on physical, emotional and spiritual development.*

- *My mission is to develop strong bonds of love with my family, to reach out to others in need, to have work I deem meaningful, to increase my knowledge, to enlarge my soul and to enhance my environment.*

You can write one mission statement that addresses your life and work as a whole, or you can write separate mission statements for each area of your life.

SECTION • ONE

Exercise Four

MY PERSONAL MISSION STATEMENT

Create your personal mission statement. Use your values pyramid to guide you. If you prefer, write separate mission statements to reflect your personal goals and your professional goals.

PERSONAL

_____

_____

_____

_____

_____

_____

_____

_____

_____

_____

_____

_____

_____

_____

_____

"Great minds have purposes; others have wishes."

—Washington Irving

Finding Your Focus

PROFESSIONAL

_____

_____

_____

_____

_____

_____

_____

_____

_____

_____

_____

_____

_____

_____

_____

_____

_____

_____

_____

_____

_____

"Change everything, except your loves."
—Voltaire

Establish Your Priorities

TAKING CONTROL TIP #6

Establish your priorities based on your values.

"He who has begun is half done. Dare to be wise: Begin."

—Horace

The individual activities you must perform to achieve the goals or vision you espoused in your mission statement are called your *priorities.* The general priorities help you decide on your more specific priorities, which makes it easy to create your To Do lists.

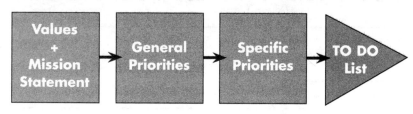

Finding Your Focus

Here's an example of how values can translate into productive days:

My Values	My Priorities		
	General	**Specific**	**To Do List**
Worship	Increase growth	Attend services	Read scriptures
Family	Spend part of day enjoying quality time	Sit down dinners and chat	Buy groceries
Intellectual Growth	Stay open to new ideas	Read books; listen to tapes; attend seminars	Select a book or tape
Adventure	Meet new people and travel to new places	Travel to Ireland and Scotland	Create travel file; phone agency
Security	Career	Work hard	Deposit checks; pay bills
Order	Improve my productivity	Clean desk	Sort articles
Personal Expression	Enhance my creativity	Write book	Write ideas for proposal
Autonomy	Be flexible	Choose time off	Decide vacation dates

SETTING PRIORITIES

"Establishing priorities and using your time well aren't things you can pick up at Harvard Business School. If you want to make good use of your time, you've got to know what's important, and then give it all you've got."

—Lee Iacocca

Exercise Five

NOW YOU TRY IT!

"Let us, then, be up and doing, With a heart for any fate; Still achieving, still pursuing, Learn to labour and to wait."

—Henry Wadsworth Longfellow

| My Values | My Priorities | | |
	General	Specific	To Do List

Finding Your Focus

<u>TAKING CONTROL TIP #7</u>

When situations come up that challenge or threaten to disrupt your time, ask questions that measure the demand against your predetermined priorities.

✔ How does this project, request, event or relationship fit in with my priorities?

✔ Is it appropriate, worth the time, energy or effort for me to get involved with this?

✔ What impact will diverting my time to this have on accomplishing other tasks or meeting other deadlines?

Don't try to get away with easy "yes/no" answers. These questions require introspection and honesty.

"My strength lies solely in my tenacity."
—Louis Pasteur

SECTION • ONE

Taking Control of Your Time

Exercise Six

MAKING DECISIONS BASED ON MY PRIORITIES

Make a decision about the following requests for involvement, ***based on your own values and priorities.*** Remember to make your decision based on your present situation.

1. Your favorite cousin asks you to attend his or her wedding to be held 1,000 miles away

I decide to:

_____

_____

_____

_____

_____

_____

_____

_____

_____

_____

_____

_____

_____

Finding Your Focus

2. The boss asks for a volunteer to be the company liaison to a community youth club. This will require two Tuesday evening meetings a month.

I decide to:

_____

_____

_____

_____

_____

_____

_____

_____

_____

_____

_____

_____

_____

"If you don't set goals for yourself, you are doomed to work to achieve the goals of somebody else."
—Brian Tracy

33

3. Your department decides to form a softball team for an interdepartmental playoff. Practice will be held on Saturday mornings for the next four months. The playoff games will be held on three consecutive Sundays.

I decide to:

_____

_____

_____

_____

_____

_____

_____

_____

_____

_____

_____

_____

_____

_____

"As is our confidence, so is our capacity."
—William Hazlitt

Finding Your Focus

Were you honest? Did you ask yourself the hard questions (see p. 31) about whether these activities/events matched your values and priorities?

The more often you're able to weigh a request for your time against your values and priorities before you say "yes," the less often you'll find your day disrupted by activities that are unimportant to you and leave you feeling rushed and disorganized. Asking these questions means you are TAKING CONTROL rather than the demands and activities taking control of you.

TAKING CONTROL TIP #8

When priorities seem difficult to set, ask yourself: Will this matter in five years? How about in one?

"Whenever you see a successful business, someone made a courageous decision."

—Peter Drucker

Do the Right Things Right

TAKING CONTROL TIP #9

Use the 80/20 rule.

In the nineteenth century, Italian economist Vilfredo Pareto noticed that 80 percent of the wealth of his country was in the hands of 20 percent of the people. Since then, this 80/20 principle has been applied to virtually all kinds of situations. Sometimes the relationship is 90/10 or 85/15, but it is surprising how often an analysis will reveal that 80/20 makes sense. Some have applied it to these situations:

- 80 percent of the sales come from 20 percent of the customers.

- 80 percent of the sick leave is taken by 20 percent of the employees.

- 80 percent of the file usage is on 20 percent of the files.

Finding Your Focus

- 80 percent of dining out is done at 20 percent of your favorite restaurants.

- 80 percent of the washing is done on 20 percent of the clothes.

- 80 percent of the work you do on a given day results in only 20 percent of goal-related accomplishments.

Finding the time to work on goal-related priority activities can be a challenge. That's because so much of our day is filled with the "trivial many" things that require attention. These activities could be called "preparation" or "maintenance" tasks that may very well relate to important goals and projects; however, the tasks in themselves only *support* the main goal. Examples of "trivial many" activities would be setting up files, ordering supplies, gathering facts or statistics for a report, networking, reading, attending planning meetings and so on. Often these support tasks occupy as much as 80 percent of your day.

Only 20 percent of our time is said to be spent on those "vital few," on-target, specific activities and tasks that bring in the business or result in true goal-related accomplishments. Examples of these might be sending out a finished proposal, posting checks, talking to a client, addressing the board or closing a deal.

TAKING CONTROL TIP #10

Don't be overcome by the routine tasks. Focus on your priorities–your goal-related activities! Place value-based activities on your daily To Do list (see p. 32).

TAKING CONTROL TIP #11

Working long hours each day isn't as important
as working on the right things.

In the process of TAKING CONTROL, it's important to
assess which are the right things for *you* to work on
at any given moment and then to do them right. You
can put in a twelve-hour day and accomplish nothing
if you spend it working on the wrong things. You've
already established what some of these right things are
by establishing your priorities. But, as discussed, there
are other daily activities pushing for your attention and
pulling at your energy, even though they may not be
high payoff or directly goal-related.

How do you achieve a balance between routine
activities and high-payoff goal-related activities?
By applying a simple formula that weighs your
important tasks against your urgent tasks:

$$I \times U = P.$$

This formula helps you take care of the right things at the right time and in the proper order. Essentially, what this formula does is help you prioritize your priorities—and shows you which tasks and activities you would be better off delegating—or dumping altogether.

The Concepts of Important and Urgent

TAKING CONTROL TIP #12

Not everything that is screaming urgent is necessarily the most important (based on values and priorities).

Finding Your Focus

In the formula I x U = P, the "I" stands for "important," and the "U" stands for "urgent."

Important things are the activities and events that bring you closer to the goals or the vision you described in your mission statement.

Urgent things demand your immediate consideration—they can't wait.

PRIORITY WORKSHEET		
Priority Rank	Today's Activities	Rank/Value X Time Value = Priority Importance ("1" is most important) 1=Urgent, Today 2=Timely, Soon 3=Flexible, Anytime OK

When you assign your activities a numerical value based on their importance and another based on their urgency and then multiply those numbers, you get a *priority value* (the "P" in the formula) you can use to rank your priorities for each day.

Taking Control of Your Time

Here's an example, based on the priorities listed in the example on page 29.

Here's an example, based on the priorities listed in the example on page 29.

> *"Each morning sees some task begin, Each evening sees it close; Something attempted, something done, Has earned a night's repose."*
>
> —Henry Wadsworth Longfellow

PRIORITY WORKSHEET

Priority Rank	Today's Activities	Rank/Value Importance ("1" is most important)	X	Time Value 1=Urgent, Today 2=Timely, Soon 3=Flexible, Anytime OK	=	Priority Value
1	Read scriptures	1	X	1	=	1
5	Buy groceries	1	X	1	=	1
4	Attend seminar	1	X	1	=	1
8	Create travel file	2	X	2	=	4
9	Phone travel agency	3	X	3	=	6
2	Deposit checks	1	X	1	=	1
3	Pay bills	1	X	1	=	1
10	Sort articles	3	X	3	=	9
7	Write ideas for book proposal	2	X	2	=	4
6	Decide on vacation dates	2	X	1	=	2

Now you try it!

Use the values and priorities you listed in Exercise 5 to complete the following Priority Worksheet.

1. In the "Today's Activities" column, list your priorities for the current day.

2. In the first column of the Priority Worksheet, rank your priorities according to their importance; with 1 being the most important.

3. In the second column of the worksheet, rank each priority according to its urgency, with 1 being something you must do today; 2 being something you must complete soon, but not necessarily today; and 3 being something you can do anytime.

4. Multiply each item's importance ranking by its urgency ranking to arrive at its priority value.

5. In the column labeled "Priority Rank," rank your priorities in the order they must be completed to achieve maximum effectiveness for the day. Note that the item with the lowest priority value will be your highest priority for the day, so it will receive a 1 in the "Priority Rank" column.

Exercise Seven

RANKING YOUR PRIORITIES

Taking Control of Your Time

PRIORITY WORKSHEET

Priority Rank	Today's Activities	Rank/Value Importance ("1" is most important)	X	Time Value 1=Urgent, Today 2=Timely, Soon 3=Flexible, Anytime OK	=	Priority Value
		_____	X	_____	=	_____
		_____	X	_____	=	_____
		_____	X	_____	=	_____
		_____	X	_____	=	_____
		_____	X	_____	=	_____
		_____	X	_____	=	_____
		_____	X	_____	=	_____
		_____	X	_____	=	_____
		_____	X	_____	=	_____
		_____	X	_____	=	_____

Finding Your Focus

As you can see from Exercise #7, your urgent activities aren't always your most important. A game you're scheduled to play in for your company team may be urgent because it's scheduled for today, but it's not as important as meeting the deadline for a critical report you must present to the board of directors today. Both activities are urgent because they must be done today, but the report is more important because it has greater consequences.

TAKING CONTROL TIP #13

Spend a few minutes each morning jotting down your day's priorities and then ranking them according to the I x U = P formula.

The few minutes you spend doing this will pay huge dividends in the form of a more focused, more organized and more productive workday.

Assigning these priorities a certain time slot each day is an excellent way to anchor them and commit to them. Taking Control Tips for scheduling your daily priorities and the tools for doing so are discussed in Chapter 3, "The Organized Person's Tool Kit."

The Organized Person's Tool Kit

It's important to have and use the right tools to help you TAKE CONTROL. You select the tools— the products and processes—to help you develop your system of organization.

TAKING CONTROL TIP #14

Develop or purchase a time management organizational system that works for you– whether it's a simple appointment calendar, a computer program (PIM/Personal Information Manager), binder-style planner with tabbed sections, a daily To Do list or a combination of these tools and others.

"Vision without action is just a dream. Action without vision just passes the time. Vision with action can change the world."

—Loren Eiseley

Don't become obsessive about getting organized. *Remember, you have to be only as organized as you need to be in order to get what you want done in the way you want.* Your organization system should assist, facilitate and advance your work, not hinder or bog you down. If you can work well with a simple To Do list or appointment calendar, there's no reason to purchase a binder-style organizer.

48

The Organized Person's Tool Kit

Appointment Calendars

There are many ways to keep track of the hours, days, months and years of your life. Just like wall calendars, appointment calendars vary in color, size, shape, style, emphasis, function and design.

Your job is to decide what you want in your calendar. Here are some major features you should consider before choosing an appointment calendar:

- Is it user-friendly?

- Is it the appropriate size for your needs? (Do you need one that sits on your desk, or one that is sized to fit in your purse, pocket or briefcase?)

- Is it readable? (Is the layout organized well? Does the size of the print guide you to the area of the page you need to focus on?)

- Does it allow enough space for you to write? (Does one day per page best suit your needs, or can you get by with one week per page?)

- Is it flexible and portable?

"How pleasant it is, at the end of the day, No follies to have to repent; But reflect on the past, and be able to say, That my time has been properly spent."

—Jane Taylor

TAKING CONTROL TIP #15

Write everything in/on your calendar in pencil. That way, if something changes, you can erase it easily. An appointment calendar with crossouts and arrows quickly becomes cluttered and you won't be able to read your scheduled activities at a glance.

Organizers

"If we triumph in the little things of our common hours, we are sure to triumph in our lives."

—Anonymous

An organizer is a portable appointment calendar and more. An organizer, for example, has a section you can use for taking notes so you don't have to remember everything or keep track of stray scraps of paper. An organizer also has sections for phone numbers and addresses, To Do lists, daily and monthly calendars and other key information so you can keep things together in one place. It also has pages for goal setting and planning so you can stay focused on your priorities and find balance in life. In short, when used properly, organizers can help you get more done and help you feel more in control.

CHAPTER • THREE

The Organized Person's Tool Kit

As you contemplate TAKING CONTROL, anticipate what you need in an organizer.

The web chart on the next page will give you an idea of some of the features available in organizers. (Later in this chapter, you'll learn how to create your own web chart as an alternative to the traditional To Do list and outline.)

**WEB CHART:
PLAN YOUR
PLANNER**

*"He trudg'd along
unknowing
what he sought,
And whistled as
he went, for want
of thought."*
—John Dryden

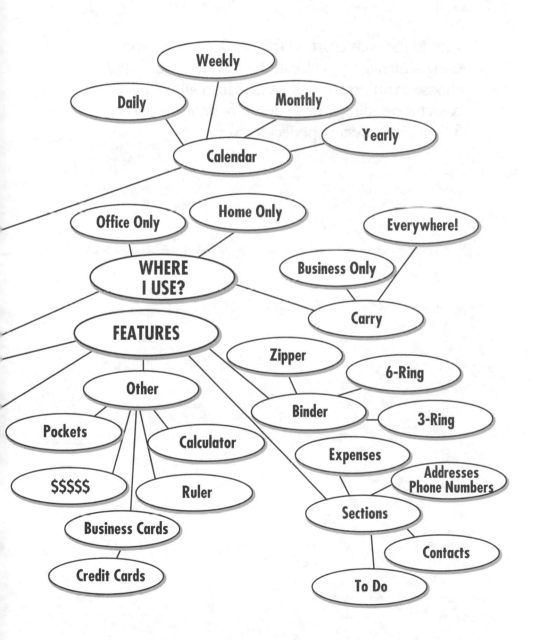

Exercise Eight

CHOOSING FEATURES FOR YOUR ORGANIZER

Turn to the web chart on the previous page, and using a highlighter, color in the features you would choose in an organizer system. This will be a good basis for deciding how to develop, improve upon or fully utilize a system perfect for you.

*"Mighty things
from small
beginnings grow."*
—John Dryden

The Organized Person's Tool Kit

To Do Lists

The To Do list is an "oldie and a goldie" idea for TAKING CONTROL. It helps to write things down. List the things you need to do so that you can then prioritize them and start working on what needs your most immediate attention.

TAKING CONTROL TIP #16

Create a *master list* of things to do.

These are projects and tasks that you must or would like to do within a certain time period, usually a week or a month. Once you've created a master list, make a daily list that draws from the items on your master list.

TAKING CONTROL TIP #17

If you know that something you've listed on your To Do list will take more than one day to finish, specify how many hours you plan to work on it for that day. For example, the item should read: "Work on *Project X* for *amount of time*."

You'll gain the most from your daily To Do lists if you keep these guidelines in mind:

"Punctuality is the politeness of kings."
—Louis XVIII

- **Write down everything you must, should, or would like to do for the day.** It's a mistake to think you can remember everything. Also, if you really want to accomplish something that's important but not urgent, put it on the list. Otherwise, time will race by, and you won't get it done.

- **Update your list each day.** Move forward items from your master list or items from the previous day that you didn't complete. It's important to adjust your list every day. Days are different. There are always variations in your routine, and priorities change.

- **Keep your list handy so you can refer to it easily.** Refer to it often during the day to stay on track.

- **Enjoy crossing each completed item off your list.** This is when your To Do list becomes your "Ta Dah" list. Enjoy and celebrate the good feeling that comes with accomplishment.

TAKING CONTROL TIP #18

Even if you work on a computer, print out a clean hard copy of your To Do list every day.

A printed copy of your To Do list is easier to keep nearby at all times. It serves as a constant reminder of what you've done and what you still need to do.

<u>**TAKING CONTROL TIP #19**</u>

Create or purchase a daily To Do list or daily planner customized for your job and life activities.

The following pages offer some examples of effective To Do list styles.

The Organized Person's Tool Kit

```
DATE_____

                    TO DO
        Task                    Priority
_____
_____
_____
_____
_____
_____
_____


                   TO SEE
   Time      Person or Group      Place
_____
_____
_____
_____
_____
_____
_____
```

**SAMPLE
FORMAT FOR
TO DO LISTS**

TO PHONE		
Person	*Reason for Call*	*Priority*

FOLLOW UP

"I have never heard anything about the resolutions of the apostles, but a great deal about their acts."
—Horace Mann

The Organized Person's Tool Kit

NAME_____	DATE_____

TO DO LIST

Task	*Done*

MEETINGS

Time	*Person or Group*	*Place*

SAMPLE DAILY PLANNER FORMAT

"Every noble activity makes room for itself."

—Ralph Waldo Emerson

SECTION • ONE

PHONE CALLS TO MAKE/ MESSAGES TO RETURN		
Person	*Phone*	*Agenda/Message*

"Things may come to those who wait, but only things left by those who hustle."
—Abraham Lincoln

The Organized Person's Tool Kit

Web Charts, Clustering, and Mind Mapping

There are many tools besides lists that can help you get organized. Work flow charts, timelines and other techniques can help you see your work in an orderly way.

Another planning technique is to create a web chart. This is sometimes called clustering or mind mapping. You can use a web chart to plan a letter, write an essay, organize a party, meeting or conference–anything.

This technique works well because you:

- Make your ideas graphically clear.
- Focus on the end goal.
- Capture ideas at random.
- See ideas in relation to others.
- Visualize the whole project.

"The difference between creative people and others is that creative people learn to pay attention to their ideas. They let their minds go with new ideas and try to take them further."

—Roger Von Oech
A Whack on the Side of the Head

Basically, creating a web chart involves putting a broad idea in a circle in the center of a page. As related ideas occur to you, simply draw a line that extends from the original circle to another circle with your new idea. You can extend spokes of ideas off the second layer of ideas until eventually you have several subpoints, or subcircles. Two different types of web charts are shown on the next two pages.

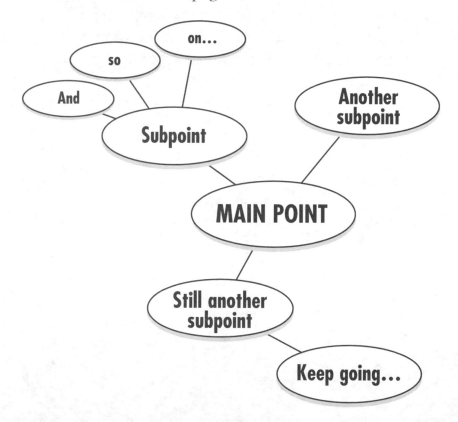

**SAMPLE WEB
CHART FOR
PACKING FOR
A TRIP**

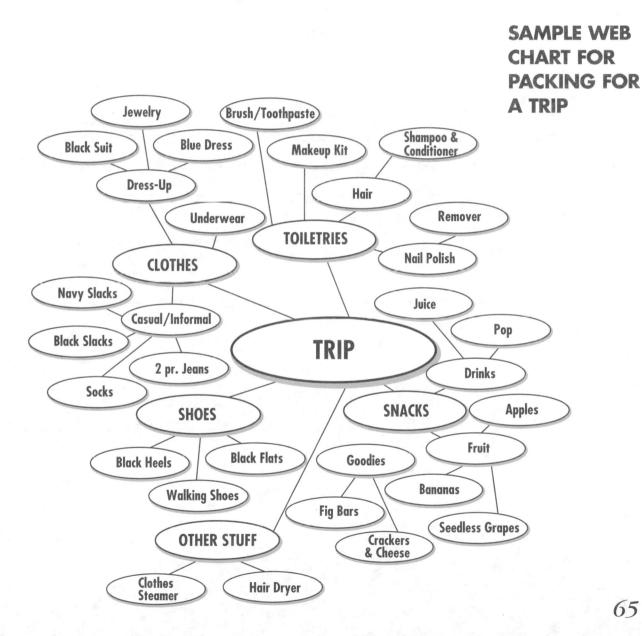

**WEB CHART
FOR AN
ANNUAL
CONFERENCE**

Another way to do it!

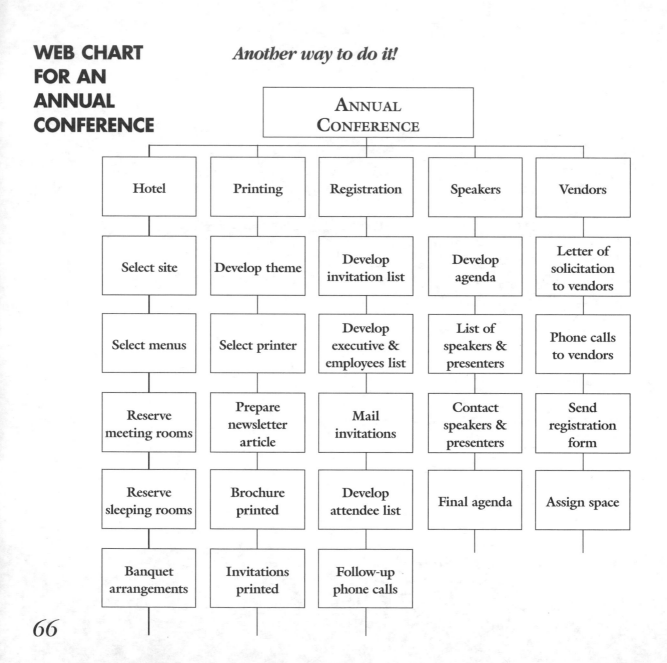

		ANNUAL CONFERENCE		
Hotel	Printing	Registration	Speakers	Vendors
Select site	Develop theme	Develop invitation list	Develop agenda	Letter of solicitation to vendors
Select menus	Select printer	Develop executive & employees list	List of speakers & presenters	Phone calls to vendors
Reserve meeting rooms	Prepare newsletter article	Mail invitations	Contact speakers & presenters	Send registration form
Reserve sleeping rooms	Brochure printed	Develop attendee list	Final agenda	Assign space
Banquet arrangements	Invitations printed	Follow-up phone calls		

TAKING CONTROL TIP #20

Make your web chart work for you.

Color in the tasks as you complete them. Or number them in order of priority. If possible, assign or delegate, some of the tasks to others. Be sure to assign due dates. Just do whatever you need to do to make your web chart work for you.

"All truly wise thoughts have been thought already thousands of times; but to make them truly ours, we must think them over again honestly, until they take root in our personal experience."
—Goethe

Exercise Nine

DEVELOP A
WEB CHART

Now you try it. Think about the individual tasks
you must complete to pull off a big project, such as
organizing the company picnic or planning a birthday
party. Put the main task in the center and create layers
of individual tasks as you think of them. Get as detailed
as you want. There's plenty of room to extend your
chart to page 69.

Company Picnic

CHAPTER • THREE

The Organized Person's Tool Kit

"Let our advance worrying become advance thinking and planning."

—Winston Churchill

"Take time to deliberate; but when the time for action arrives, stop thinking and go in."

—Andrew Jackson

Important Prioritizing and Scheduling Tips

Whether you choose an organizer, a simple To Do list, or a web chart to take control of the tasks you must accomplish each day, you cannot overlook the importance of scheduling those tasks and activities. It does no good to write down your activities and then plunge into them without considering which ones to do first and the best time of day to do them.

TAKING CONTROL TIP #21

Spend ten to fifteen minutes in the morning planning your day.

This is the most important part of your day. Planning sets the tone and determines what you'll work on during the day.

The Organized Person's Tool Kit

TAKING CONTROL TIP #22

Work on your priorities first.

For true productivity, you must work on your most important items first. The top priorities have a sense of urgency. Next focus in on the items that are also important, but not as urgent. Finally, schedule some time for the items that would be nice to do. These things usually are easier, quicker and more fun; however, don't get fooled into thinking that if you accomplish twenty-seven of these low-priority items that you've had a productive day. It's the *quality* (priority) of the item that counts in TAKING CONTROL, not *quantity*. Remember, too, that even your priorities have priorities. You can do only one thing at a time. (See Chapter 2 for details on setting priorities.)

"We cannot do everything at once, but we can do something at once."
—Calvin Coolidge

TAKING CONTROL TIP #23

Avoid panic and stress: Don't schedule every minute of your day.

Your day must be flexible. Put time-related activities, such as appointments and meetings, on your calendar. Then select tasks from your To Do list or master list to flesh out your day. Be sure to leave room on your schedule for unexpected interruptions or crises.

TAKING CONTROL TIP #24

Budget time the way you budget your money!

Allow a certain amount of time for completing each task. Set a timer when you start. The alarm saves you from tasks you don't like to do and pulls you from jobs you like and would spend too much time on.

Taking Control of Three Common Time Wasters

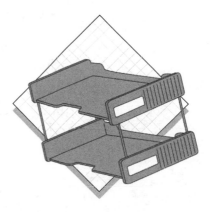

No amount of prioritizing will do you any good if you allow time wasters to creep into your day. Time wasters will eat up the time you've allotted for your activities, and you'll find yourself doing one of two things:

- Abandoning one activity while it's still incomplete because it's time to move on to the next item on your list.

- Taking more time than you've allotted for an activity and pushing everything else on your list back.

"Without a deadline, baby, I wouldn't do nothin'."

—Duke Ellington

Either way, all you'll have to show for your day is a piece of paper with a nice list of ranked priorities— that you didn't follow through on!

Three of the most common time wasters are:

- Perfectionism.

- Procrastination.

- Mouse-milking.

A fourth time waster is personal disorganization, but it includes so many different areas that it's included as a separate section. Read Section 2 to get a grip on such things as clutter, your office, your reading material and your computer files.

Perfectionism

Sometimes *good* is good enough! If your standards are too high, they may be impossible to reach and, thus, discourage you from getting anything done, including getting organized.

Why do we take on a task and try to do it "perfectly"?

- We enjoy doing it.

- We have the time, so we fill it.

- We're nervous about it, so we keep working at it.

- We're getting paid to do it, so we feel we better keep making "improvements."

- We have a "reputation" to keep up, even if no money is involved.

- We're not sure when it's finished, so we keep fiddling with it.

"As if you could kill time without injuring eternity."
—Henry David Thoreau

Taking Control of Your Time

TAKING CONTROL TIP #25

Know when to stop working on a task.

"Often done is good enough."

—Old Saying

When you feel yourself in a "perfectionistic" mood, ask yourself these questions:

- Will the results be substantially better if I put in more effort?

- Will I get paid more?

- Would anyone else notice the improvements? (Or would anyone else care?)

- Have I gone as far as I can without getting help?

- Have I already done more than is expected of me?

Your answer is the key to whether you should keep at the task, or just STOP!

CHAPTER • FOUR

Taking Control of Three Common Time Wasters

Procrastination

Procrastination is delaying. It is putting something off until tomorrow or later. Sometimes people put things off because circumstances change: a more important priority comes up and must be dealt with. Generally, though, we procrastinate on a task for these reasons:

- It will take a long time, and there's not a solid block of time to complete it.

- It will take a long time, and that in itself is so overwhelming that we avoid the task.

- It's complicated.

- It requires quiet time.

- It requires too much energy.

- It's difficult.

- The tools needed to complete it aren't easily accessible.

- It's uncomfortable to do.

- It might hurt.

- It costs too much.

- We've already put it off for too long.

"The best time to plant a tree was 20 years ago. The second best time is now."

—Ancient proverb

TAKING CONTROL TIP #26

The key to overcoming procrastination is to put the task in perspective.

Here are some questions that will help:
- What's the worst thing that could happen if I *never* did this?

- What's the worst thing that could happen if I *stalled* an hour? a day? a week? a year?

- Can I live with the worst happening?

If you decide you *can* live without completing the task, then drop it. No guilt. Sometimes the time we spend worrying about doing something is more of an energy-drainer than doing the task itself.

If you ask yourself these questions and decide the task really must be addressed, then you have three options:

- Do it yourself. Schedule it and make a sincere commitment to getting it done.

- Delegate it.

- Hire someone to do it.

"How come there is never enough time to do something right the first time, but there is always time to do it again?"

—Anonymous

CHAPTER • FOUR

Taking Control of Three Common Time Wasters

Mouse-milking

Have you ever tried to milk a mouse? Not literally, of course. Mouse-milking refers to certain activities that at the moment are a waste of time. Don't confuse this with much-needed recreation or stress-relieving activities. Mouse-milking doesn't refer to pursuing a hobby or an avocation. It refers to a task or project that is a waste of time when measured against your priorities.

Here are five common ways to mouse-milk:

- Doing a task you could easily delegate

- Doing a task too well

- Taking too long to complete a task

- Doing a task that keeps you from a greater priority

- Doing a task that saves you from a dreaded priority

"There is a difference between striving for excellence, and striving for perfection. The first is attainable, gratifying and healthy. The second is unattainable, frustrating and neurotic. It is also a terrible waste of time."

—Edwin Bliss

Exercise Ten

IDENTIFYING MY MOUSE-MILKERS

Check off any mouse-milkers you do yourself. Add any that you don't see here. Be honest!

Remember, there's no point doing well what you shouldn't be doing at all.

☐ Untangling paper clips

☐ Arranging my paper clips, pens and pencils, and other items by size and color

☐ Wrapping my rubber bands into a ball

☐ Arranging and rearranging my refrigerator magnets

☐ Putting reinforcements on every page in a three-ring binder

☐ Reading the out-of-date catalogs I find as I sort stuff

CHAPTER • FOUR

Taking Control of Three Common Time Wasters

I admit it. Here are my favorite mouse-milkers:

_____

_____

_____

_____

_____

_____

_____

_____

_____

_____

_____

_____

_____

_____

_____

_____

_____

_____

_____

_____

"Procrastination is a close relative of incompetence and a handmaiden of inefficiency."
—Alec MacKenzie,
The Time Trap

TAKING CONTROL TIP #27

As you discover yourself mouse-milking, stop and ask whether you're trying to avoid a more important task.

You'll be surprised at how becoming aware of your mouse-milking habits and putting an end to them will give you the "free time" you've been waiting for to start something you really want to accomplish.

Honesty here is the ticket to TAKING CONTROL.

"There are three things extremely hard: steel, a diamond, and to know one's self."
—Ben Franklin

Overcoming Personal Disorganization

Finding Your Organizational Style

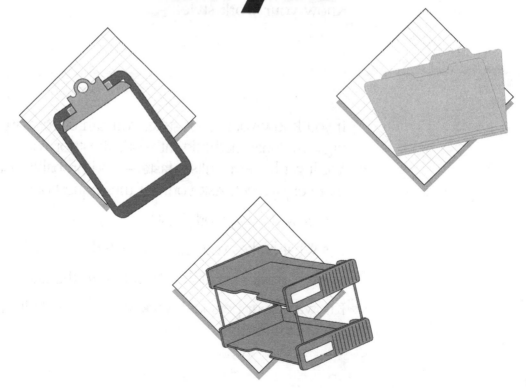

SECTION • TWO

Overcoming Personal Disorganization

Style your work and work your style. Before you tackle specific areas of your life that may be disorganized, take a minute to gain an understanding of your work style and your organizational style. There are different ways to get a job done, and that's certainly true of the job of organizing.

TAKING CONTROL TIP #28

Know your work style.

If you know your work style, you can choose an organizational method that works best for you. You'll get better results—faster—and probably with more enjoyment. Ask yourself these questions:

- How do you work best?

- What makes you feel committed to a task?

- What helps you follow through to the end?

Knowing your personal work style can be half the job of organizing.

The O-and-O (Overview and Organize) Style

In the O-and-O style, you think about the job and mentally analyze the process. The key characteristic of this style is *planning.* You may do the planning formally, or you may take a more casual approach:

- Gaze out the window or sit down and do the planning in your head.

- Make lists or work progress charts.

- Take measurements.

- Count the cost in time and/or money.

Once you have your plan in place, then and only then do you start organizing.

Advantage: You get an overview of what the task involves and can be very realistic about the effort and time necessary to complete the task.

Disadvantage: You may tend to feel overwhelmed and stop at the planning stage.

"Let us watch well our beginnings and results will manage themselves."
—Alexander Clark

The Sneak-Up-On-It Style

With this style, you work on the edges first. You ease into the job because you need time to adjust to the idea of it. You work on fringe tasks that help you get ready to work on the job itself. You may do some of the following:

- Clean your desk before you start something new

- Sharpen your pencils

- Organize your tools

- Finish another quick project

- Listen to music that puts you in the mood to complete the task

- Tidy the area around your workplace and eliminate distractions

- Type any words that come to your mind and then gradually get focused

Finally, when you've cleared the decks and the cobwebs, you *start.*

"What we call the beginning is often the end. And to make an end is to make a beginning. The end is where we start from."

—T.S. Eliot

Advantage: You prepare your environment to eliminate distractions, or you slowly move your mind to focus on the task at hand.

Disadvantage: You may bog down in the sneaking-up-on-it stage and not get to the main effort very quickly. You may be mouse-milking (see Chapter 4). Some people might consider all this fuss of getting ready to work as being nothing more than busy work–or even stalling–but some people need to get into the proper mental and emotional state as a prelude to working on a specific task.

A-Little-At-a-Time Style

You don't want to burn out while you're working on a project. To avoid doing so, you can take small steps that move the project forward–nothing big or dramatic–just some efforts to put yourself in a better position to tackle the task.

For the Little-at-a-Time style, you might do things like these:

- Divide up photos by year and place them in large envelopes

- Bring all the parts of the project together into one place

- Get out all your sales receipts and divide them into business and personal expenses

- Put all the items you've wanted to read "when you get around to it" in one place

- Scratch a few notes on a legal pad as you think of ideas

Advantage: You get a portion (however small) of the task completed, which gives you a sense of accomplishment. This method is similar to the "divide and conquer" strategy suggested for controlling clutter (see Chapter 7), but it applies to more areas than organizing clutter.

Disadvantage: You get discouraged because the positive changes come in such small, incremental steps that you feel the job isn't really getting done.

Finding Your Organizational Style

Jump-In Style

With the Jump-In style, you just dive in and get going on the job. You get a burst of energy and begin. For example, you might just jump in and start working on any one of these tasks:

- Make a scrapbook, sorting as you go

- Write a letter, essay or proposal without following an outline

- Open your suitcase and throw things in as you think of them

- Clean the garage, starting with the first thing you trip over

- Dust, label and arrange all the items in a collection you may have

Advantage: You throw yourself into the effort and finally do something! You may get lucky and exceed your expectations and really move the job along, making it easy to come back and do more, or you may actually finish!

Disadvantage: You may burn out more quickly. You may find that you bite off more than you can chew and stop in the middle of the job. In this case, you may leave things in greater disarray than they were before you started.

"Do not wait; the time will never be 'just right.' Start where you stand, and work with whatever tools you may have at your command, and better tools will be found as you go along."

—Napoleon Hill

91

TAKING CONTROL TIP #29

Realize that the style you choose may not only depend on your preferred work style, but also on the task to be completed.

For example, you might use the O-and-O approach if you were going to give a twenty-five minute speech to forty members of your local chamber of commerce, go on a week's vacation, give your boss a proposal for a new employee recognition program or write a letter of apology to a client. On the other hand, you might choose to just "jump in" and wash the car or clean the garage.

"In life, as in chess, forethought wins."

—Charles Buxton

Finding Your Organizational Style

On the lines below, write down several tasks (clean closets, write procedures manual, etc.) you must tackle in the next few weeks. Then choose an organizational style that would work best to complete it.

Task/Project

_____

_____

_____

_____

_____

_____

_____

_____

_____

_____

_____

_____

_____

Work Style

_____

_____

_____

_____

_____

_____

_____

_____

_____

_____

_____

_____

_____

Exercise Eleven

FINDING THE OPTIMUM ORGANIZATIONAL STYLE

"Work expands so as to fill the time available for its completion."

—C. Northcote Parkinson

93

Making Your Work Space Work for You

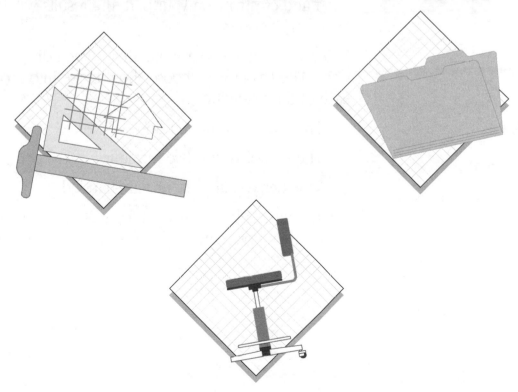

SECTION • TWO

Overcoming Personal Disorganization

You respond to your environment. How you arrange your work space influences *how* you work, how *fast* you work, your work *routine* and how you *feel* when you're in your space. Without a doubt, organizing your work space increases your productivity.

The goal is to create a space that is efficient, comfortable and personal. It is possible to create a work space that is both aesthetically pleasing and functionally effective. Although it will take extra effort and creativity on your part, the results will be extremely satisfying.

You can configure your work area several different ways. The layout you choose should take into account each of the following:

- The type of work you do
- The size of your office furniture
- Whether you are left- or right-handed
- The atmosphere you want to create for visitors, including placement of chairs

Making Your Work Space Work for You

- Proper lighting
- Some control of noise level, traffic flow, distractions
- Adequate work space and work surfaces
- Adequate and handy storage space
- Comfortable chair
- Handy placement of tools and equipment (telephone, computer, files and so on)
- A paper flow system that emphasizes action

"Studious of elegance and ease, Myself alone I seek to please."
—John Gay

Overcoming Personal Disorganization

Your Work Space and Your Desk

TAKING CONTROL TIP #30

Your desk is your primary and prime work area; therefore, it should be as organized as it needs to be for you to get your work done.

Read that again: as organized as it needs to be to get your work done. People differ in the level of "tidiness" they require or prefer to be productive. You may be the type who finds a clean desk too sterile. You may need a photo or a pencil holder or other knick-knacks or tools to create an inviting environment. That's fine, as long as these items don't distract you, interfere with your work, or add to the clutter. Remember, your desktop is not a storage area. (See Exercise 14, p. 112, "Analyzing My Work Space.")

Making Your Work Space Work for You

TAKING CONTROL TIP #31

Use two work surfaces.

Some people find they can work more efficiently if they have a primary area where they do most of their work and a secondary area called a *return.* Sit in your office chair. Look around at your work area and ask:

- Do I have enough open space to effectively work on a project? If not, why? Do I really need a second work surface, or do I simply need to make better use of the one I have?

  - *For example:* Are papers from another project still lying around, unfiled? If so, finish the project or pull it together and file it.

  - Is my work space unnecessarily cluttered by items I keep out for display? If so, read Taking Control Tip #32.

- Do I have a work surface that is simply inadequate for my work needs? If so, see what you can do to bring in and set up an additional surface, even a fold-up table for a current need.

> *"Change is not made without inconvenience, even from worse to better."*
>
> —John Hooker

SECTION • TWO

Overcoming Personal Disorganization

TAKING CONTROL TIP #32

Minimize the number of things around you; keep out just what you need.

"A place for everything, and everything in its place."

—Samuel Smiles

Airplane pilots have their work space wrapped around them. Chefs have all their pots and pans and ingredients at hand. It's true: a work space works best when things that you normally need are within an easy *reach radius.*

The challenge is to decide exactly which items you really need handy to do your work. Not everything has to be at your fingertips. If you kept *everything* within easy reach, your work area would also be your storage area. Here's a handy guide for where you might store items based on how often you use them:

Use	Location
Daily	On top of primary work area
Weekly	Inside desk
Monthly	In same room
Less than monthly	In another room

Making Your Work Space Work for You

Sit in your chair and check what is within arm's reach. Can you reach your key items without much effort? Stretch your arms out, touch each item, and ask:

- Is this item for looks or to use?

- How often do I use this?

If you can honestly say you use it or want it enough to have it taking up space in such a valuable, prime area, then keep it there. If your answer leaves some doubt, take the item off your desk and store it. You'll soon find out whether you miss it.

Exercise Twelve

IS IT CLUTTER OR AN ESSENTIAL TOOL?

TAKING CONTROL TIP #33

Create a system that truly accommodates and facilitates the flow of paper.

Sit in your desk chair. Do you see a clear paper flow path? Can you follow a piece of paper from its point of entry in your office to the decision point. See Chapter 8 for tips on controlling paper.

TAKING CONTROL TIP #34

Establish a message system that *works.*

Create a definite, consistent place where written messages can be placed when you aren't in your office. Make sure your message center is easy for the person delivering the message to find and easy for you to see.

CHAPTER • SIX

Making Your Work Space Work for You

TAKING CONTROL TIP #35

Plan the location of your desk and chair so that you can't be easily distracted or interrupted.

If you place your desk and chair so you're facing your door or an outside window, you'll find yourself paying more attention to what's going on outside your office rather than on your work. Likewise, if you place your desk near your door or elsewhere in your office where it's easy for people in the hallway to make eye contact, you're inviting drop-in visitors.

Another way to discourage drop-in visitors is to place extra chairs where they aren't easily accessible. You can always move these chairs to a more convenient location when you're expecting visitors.

"Before I was a genius, I was a drudge."
—Jan Paderewski

TAKING CONTROL TIP #36

Use modular office furniture.

It offers you the most flexible layouts. Here are some typical work area layouts:

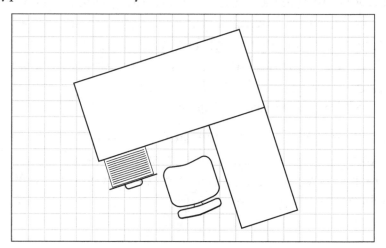

L-shape: Desk with a return.

This is a standard desk arrangement. The return is usually slightly lower than the desk and can be to the left or right of your main work area.

Making Your Work Space Work for You

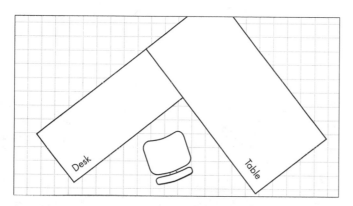

L-shape: Desk with table at right angle.

Unlike a return, all surfaces can be the same height.
The far, front corner of the table is not as accessible
when you're sitting in your desk chair.

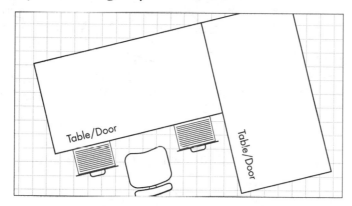

L-shape: Two tables or doors placed at right angles.

For an inexpensive and large work surface, you could
use a plain, well-sanded and varnished door supported
by a couple of two-drawer file cabinets.

105

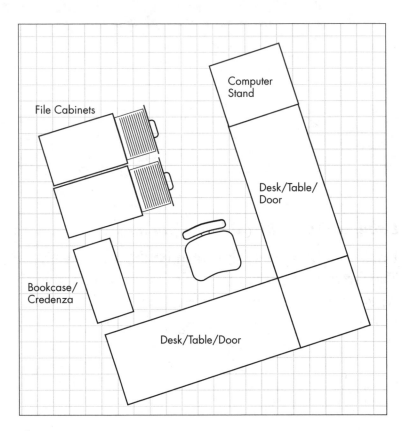

J-shape.

The J-shape layout works well if you have a large amount of furniture.

Making Your Work Space Work for You

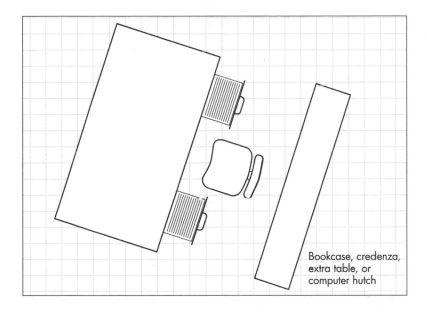

Bookcase, credenza, extra table, or computer hutch

Parallel-shape.

The parallel layout provides you with easy access to additional files, books and other materials you may not want to keep on your desk. If you have a swivel chair, particularly, all you need to do is turn your chair to grab what you need.

Remember: No matter what arrangement you choose, the placement of the visitor's chair in relationship to where you sit establishes the atmosphere of your office. Some seating arrangements, for example, give you more power. This is called *proxemics,* the study of how spatial arrangements affect personal relationships.

"Is your desk a prison where you're grueling or a garden where you're blooming?"—Anonymous

107

TAKING CONTROL TIP #37

Supplement the lighting in your office, if necessary.

Buy a desk lamp if the overhead lighting isn't sufficient. Eye strain will make you tired and less productive.

TAKING CONTROL TIP #38

Make sure your office chair is comfortable.

If your office chair isn't comfortable, you'll look for reasons to get up and move around, and you won't get much accomplished. After all, no one wants to spend eight hours in a chair that contributes to backache, bad posture, or carpal tunnel syndrome. Do Exercise 13 on the next page to find out whether your chair is a help or a hindrance.

Making Your Work Space Work for You

Sit in your chair at your desk. Be honest about how you feel in your chair.

Check (√) the following points:

Exercise Thirteen

CHECK THE SEAT OF POWER

	Poor?	Good?	Excellent!	Need Change?
Wheels				
Seat cushion padding				
Support to back				
Angle of seat back				
Height of seat back				
Legroom at desk				
Height of desk relative to chair				
Height of seat to floor				
Armrests				
Upholstery				
Color				

This is serious! If you've checked three or more categories as "Poor," you have a problem chair. Go shopping. A good office chair is one of the best investments you can make.

Personalizing Your Work Space

TAKING CONTROL TIP #39

Find a balance between personalizing your
work area and minimizing distractions.

Personalizing your work space is nothing more than
making the space look like *you* work there. No one
can tell you which items to keep around or take away.
Just be sure that whatever you do keep in your work
space doesn't interfere with your work. Distractions
can increase exponentially according to the number
of doodads sitting around in your work area.

To find out whether you've struck a balance between
personalizing your work area and minimizing
distractions, examine each item on or in your work
area and ask yourself these questions:

- Is it too large or does it take up too much space?

- Is it so small it gets lost or swept off surfaces?

Making Your Work Space Work for You

- Is it too fragile? Are you afraid it might get broken?

- Is it distracting? Do you find yourself playing with it, working around it, or otherwise fussing with it?

Pivotal question: Am I happier if I have this item near me?

Now, using what you know about creating a functional and personal work space, evaluate your own work space by answering the questions in Exercise 14.

SECTION • TWO

Overcoming Personal Disorganization

Answer "true" or "false" to the following statements.

Exercise Fourteen

ANALYZING MY WORK SPACE

True   False

1. I like the arrangement of my office. ☐ ☐

2. I feel comfortable and effective when I have visitors. ☐ ☐

3. It is difficult for something or someone to distract me from my work. ☐ ☐

4. All my work surfaces are available for work. They aren't just a place to collect and pile things. ☐ ☐

5. I have sufficient storage space for items I don't use frequently, and this space is easily accessible. ☐ ☐

"Have nothing in your house that you do not know to be useful or believe to be beautiful."

—Henry David Thoreau

6. I can easily create privacy when I need it. ☐ ☐

7. I can control the noise level. ☐ ☐

8. My work area is sufficiently lighted. ☐ ☐

9. I can reach my work area in a reasonable length of time. ☐ ☐

112

Making Your Work Space Work for You

10. I am close enough to colleagues to draw on their help when I need it. ☐ ☐

11. I have easy access to services I might need (e.g., copy machine, vendors, suppliers, supplies, equipment, restaurants). ☐ ☐

12. I can easily reach, get in touch with, and serve my clients, customers or patients. ☐ ☐

If you answered false to *any* of these statements, then you have some specific areas to focus on for improving and organizing your work space.

What to Do About Clutter

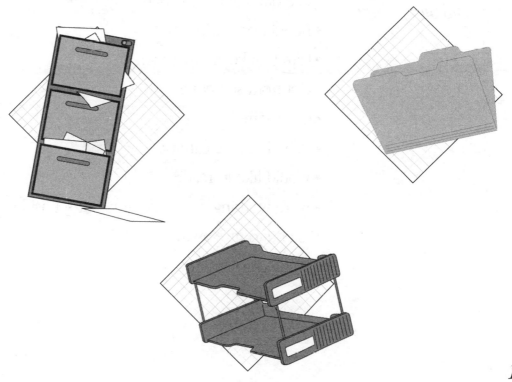

At the core of all clutter are things—trinkets, paper, souvenirs, books, household items and so on—that are either no longer needed or are needed but disorganized.

Where Clutter Comes From and Why It Stays

"Cultivate peace and harmony with all."

—George Washington

Clutter comes from things you:

- Use often and don't put away.
- Bought on a trip.
- Plan to take another look at.
- Got from someone else.
- Got for free.
- Intend to take care of.
- Would like to read.
- Were working on at one time but set aside.
- Intend to give away.
- Want to show someone.

What to Do About Clutter

- Don't know what to do with.

- Feel nostalgic and sentimental about.

- Intend to fix.

- Could use to fix something else.

- Save that "might" be worth money.

The point of such a long list is that clutter comes from numerous sources and can therefore quickly accumulate if you don't keep on top of it.

Clutter stays because you:

- Don't know where to file it or put it away.

- Are overwhelmed by the thought of hauling it out and sorting through it.

- Might need it again soon.

- Think someone else will need it.

- Were interrupted and never got back to it.

- Don't have any other place for it.

- Remember when you couldn't afford to buy it.

"Never buy anything you do not want, because it is cheap."

—Thomas Jefferson

- Have gotten used to it and don't even notice it anymore.

- Haven't decided what to do with it.

- Might have a use for it someday.

How to Stop Clutter in Its Tracks

TAKING CONTROL TIP #40

Get rid of it—now.

The best way to keep clutter at bay is to throw things out before they have a chance to accumulate. And keep this in mind: stuff often accumulates according to the space allotted to it. When you're wondering whether to keep an item or throw it out or give it away, use this seven-point keeper test:

1. Does it work—and do I use it and like it?

What to Do About Clutter

2. Can I afford to buy a new one if I decide later that I really do need it?

3. Would I regret it later if I threw it out?

4. Should I keep it for posterity?

5. Is it valuable or historical?

6. Would it be difficult or impossible to replace?

7. Do I just *want* to keep it, *and* do I have enough space to store it?

Here are some instances when you definitely *shouldn't* keep an item:

- If you forgot you had it and bought a new one.

- If it's been in storage and unneeded and unused for years.

- If you've forgotten how to play it, work it, use it.

- If you can't get spare parts to fix it.

- If you wouldn't fix it even if you *had* the spare parts.

- If it's an extra among other extras (just in case).

- If you used it for an abandoned interest, hobby or sport.

- If it's something large and low-tech that you've replaced with something small and high-tech.

- If it takes time, effort and care to maintain, and you don't care anymore.

- If you're keeping it only because it seems to be the thing to do.

- If you're keeping it only because someone said, "You don't see many of those anymore."

TAKING CONTROL TIP #41

Create a central message center.

Keep it well stocked with items needed for taking and leaving messages—notepads, pens, pencils and so on. Keeping all your messages in one place stops pads of paper, stray messages and pens and pencils from accumulating all over your house or work area.

CHAPTER • SEVEN

What to Do About Clutter

TAKING CONTROL TIP #42

Take a look at the places where clutter congregates, both at home and at work. If these places really are handy drop-off spots, why fight nature? Plan for the stuff by keeping containers nearby.

- Keep a container for nuts, bolts, washers, screws and pieces of this and that. Put the container by the phone to periodically sort and sift during long calls.

- Label a box or plastic container for things "to repair." Choose a size that will accommodate things you normally repair yourself. When you do get out the glue, glue gun and other tools, you'll have all the items in one place!

- Designate a box as a "giveaway" box. Keep it handy for items that you no longer need or want. When the box is full, place the items in plastic bags and give them to your favorite charity.

• Look at the containers that seem to attract the most clutter. Are they too large for the items that really need to be there? If the containers themselves seem to invite clutter, get smaller ones or eliminate them altogether.

TAKING CONTROL TIP #43

Take twenty, or even ten, minutes each day to zoom through the house and put things back in the right room.

When you're in those rooms again, put the things you dropped off in their proper places.

TAKING CONTROL TIP #44

Skip the souvenirs when you travel.

Take a photo or buy a postcard. Doodads not only add to the clutter, they also take time to dust.

What to Do About Clutter

TAKING CONTROL TIP #45

Use trash cans that can hold something.

Tiny, decorative ones look great, but they don't
do the job.

TAKING CONTROL TIP #46

Beware of bulletin boards.

They often attract stuff that just hangs around. Limit
bulletin boards to information that several people
may need to see: schedules, important notices, rosters
and so on.

123

TAKING CONTROL TIP #47

Junk your junk mail, unopened.

There's no reason to open junk mail. It has a certain look, so you know it when you see it. Better yet, have your name removed from mailing lists:

Register on-line at *www.dmaconsumers.org*

or write to:

DMA Mail Preference Service
Box 643
Carmel, NY 10512-0643

TAKING CONTROL TIP #48

Cancel subscriptions to magazines you never have a chance to read. Know thyself.

What to Do About Clutter

TAKING CONTROL TIP #49

Take a cue from the promoters and schedule a company-wide or family clean-up day.

Schedule a Clean Dresser Drawers Day, Jewelry Box Sparkle Session, Sports Equipment Cleanup Marathon, Clutter Control Day or Un-Packrat Day. If you really can't afford to devote an entire day to the task, set aside a few hours. Make it a fun but serious, down-and-dirty day of cleanup and clean out. Afterwards, have a party and hand out creative prizes to everyone in the office, or take the family out for pizza or ice cream. The point is to reward yourself for your hard work.

"We work to become, not to acquire."
—Elbert Hubbard

Weeding Through Clutter

As mentioned, clutter often results from failing to put away things that you use everyday. After awhile, so much accumulates that trying to get it organized is a daunting task. And most of us can't afford to dedicate one whole summer or vacation to getting organized in every aspect of our lives.

TAKING CONTROL TIP #50

The key to conquering clutter and getting organized is to "divide and conquer."

"Start by doing what's necessary, then what's possible, and suddenly you are doing the impossible."

—St. Francis of Assisi

Select small tasks that you know you can accomplish within a short period. Your progress will give you a sense of accomplishment and will provide you with incentive for moving on to the next stage of organization.

Here's how to *divide* and *divide* and *divide* and conquer:

1. Focus on an area you want to organize.

2. Divide the job into tasks. And then divide it again—and then again! Now you have a job you can tackle and finish within a reasonable amount of time.

For example, "I want to organize my _____ ":

- Bedroom (oops, too grandiose).

- Closet (pretty ambitious).

- Clothes (still daunting).

- Shoes (ah, yes, I know I can get that done!).

3. Then do it!

   Try on all your shoes. Sort them according to three categories:

   - **Keepers–good condition.** These are the shoes you wear or will wear now that you've found them. Line them up so they are easy to get to and put away.

   - **Keepers–need repair.** These are the shoes you can't wear until you have them repaired. Put them in a sack by the front door so you'll remember to drop them off at a shoe repair shop.

   - **Losers–lose them.** You'll never wear these shoes because you don't like them, they're out of style or they don't fit. Put them in a sack marked "Give Away" and drop it off at your favorite charity. Better yet, call the charity and leave the sack on the porch to be picked up.

   Follow the same steps for breaking down any project, whether at home or at work.

Divide and divide and conquer!

Here are some more examples:

Grandiose	Garage
Great	Work area
Good	Tools
Go for it	Size and separate nuts and bolts

Grandiose	House
Great	Den
Good	Bookshelves
Go for it	Dust and rearrange one bookshelf

Grandiose	Car
Great	Trunk
Good	Emergency equipment
Go for it	Restock flares and flashlight batteries

Grandiose	Yard work
Great	Front yard
Good	Shrubs
Go for it	Trim plants around front porch

What to Do About Clutter

More divide and divide and conquer...

Grandiose ...... Office, home

Great .... Files

Good .... Important files

Go for it .... Create, clean or update files for several areas (e.g., insurance, health claims, birth certificates)

Grandiose ...... Family

Great .... Kitchen phone area

Good .... Bulletin board

Go for it .... Consolidate important phone numbers

Grandiose ...... Kids

Great .... Play area

Good .... Toy box

Go for it .... Separate action figures into separate containers

"Nothing is particularly hard if you divide it into small jobs."

—Henry Ford

Exercise Fifteen

DIVIDE AND
DIVIDE AND
DIVIDE AND
CONQUER

Now you try it.

Break the following jobs down, down, down.

Kitchen

Grandiose _____

Great _____

Good_____

Go for it _____

Photo Albums

Grandiose _____

Great _____

Good_____

Go for it _____

Tax Preparation

Grandiose _____

Great _____

Good_____

Go for it _____

130

What to Do About Clutter

Hall Closet

Grandiose _____

Great _____

Good_____

Go for it _____

Audio and Videotapes

Grandiose _____

Great _____

Good_____

Go for it _____

Sports Equipment

Grandiose _____

Great _____

Good_____

Go for it _____

**MORE DIVIDE
AND DIVIDE
AND DIVIDE
AND
CONQUER**

*"...Persistence and
determination
alone are
omnipotent. The
slogan, 'press on'
has solved, and
will always solve,
the problems of
the human race."*
—Calvin Coolidge

Jewelry

Grandiose _____

Great _____

Good_____

Go for it _____

Office Supplies

Grandiose _____

Great _____

Good_____

Go for it _____

Business Contact List

Grandiose _____

Great _____

Good_____

Go for it _____

What to Do About Clutter

Project Report

Grandiose _____

Great _____

Good_____

Go for it _____

Who Says This Is a Paperless Society?

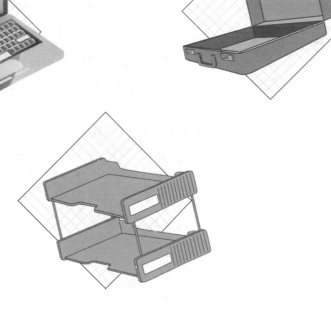

Keeping Papers From Accumulating

As you arrange your work space, one of your prime considerations must be to create a system that lets you move paper along as quickly as possible. That will help you conquer paper clutter.

You can do three things with paper:

1. **Do it.** (You will handle it.) Each time you receive a piece of paper, think about what you could do with it. Read it? file it? edit it? write on it? draw on it?

   Where you place the piece of paper will depend on two things:

   • What you decide to do with it

   • What priority you give to doing it

2. **Delegate it.** (Someone else will handle it.) Find a separate place to put papers you intend to pass on to others. If you have a few key people to whom you often distribute paperwork, keep a separate file or stack box for each of those people as well as a general or miscellaneous stack for others.

"Don't be the slave of your in-box. Just because something's there doesn't mean you have to do it."
—Malcolm Forbes

136

Who Says This Is a Paperless Society?

3. **Dump it.** (You get rid of it.) Pushing paper around from pile to pile wastes time and energy. All you're doing is circulating the clutter; it never really leaves. Instead of shuffling it, throw it away, recycle it or shred it.

How can you be sure which of the three actions you should take? Ask the paper clutter questions in Taking Control Tip #51.

"What the world really needs is more love and less paperwork."

—Pearl Bailey

TAKING CONTROL TIP #51

Hold the paper in your hand and ask the paper clutter questions.

C Copy or original?

L Likely I'll need it?

U Understandable and/or quotable?

T Timely, timeless or dated?

T Time to read it?

E Elsewhere available?

R Relevant to my work or life?

When you *should* keep paperwork:

- When the law requires it

- When it would be difficult to replace quickly

- When it's the only copy

- When it's an important item for a customer, client or project

How to Organize Your Papers

TAKING CONTROL TIP #52

Start *now* to conquer any paperwork that's been accumulating. The longer you wait to begin, the bigger the stack you'll have to purge will be.

You've learned the tips for keeping paper clutter from accumulating, but you're probably wondering what to do with the mountain of paperwork that's already

Who Says This Is a Paperless Society?

grown out of control. Here are three approaches you can take:

1. For Starters

2. For More Serious

3. For Super Serious

The one you choose will depend on how much time you have and how committed you are to getting to the bottom of the pile.

1. "For Starters"

This level of paper processing is ideal for:

- Timid "take controllers."

- Huge piles.

- When you have only enough time for a quick run-through and aren't in the mood to make terribly tough decisions.

Go through the papers very quickly, making separate piles or using different boxes/baskets for these categories:

- **To Do.** Don't think about what action you need to take. The papers you put in this pile are papers you know you must do something with.

- **To File.** These are papers that don't require any action except filing.

- **To Toss.** Keep the trash can handy for papers that are obvious throwaways.

2. "For More Serious"

Paper processing at this level is effective for:

- Sorting medium-sized piles.

- Basic, nothing-fancy organizing.

- Narrowing the stack down according to more specific actions to be taken.

Sort the papers into five piles:

- **To Do.** At this level of processing, you'll still encounter many papers that you won't want to make a specific decision about. Use the "To Do" pile for items that require action and that you'll further sort later.

- **To Read.** Place articles, reports, newspaper clippings and so on that you haven't had time to read in this pile. You'll learn tips for conquering your "To Read" pile later in this chapter.

- **To File.** Again, place here any items that need to be filed.

- **To Refer To.** This is a pile for papers that you need to refer to often, so you don't want to place them in the traditional file cabinet. Later in this chapter you'll explore some alternatives, such as "tickler files," for storing these papers but keeping them handy.

- **To Toss.** Get out the old circular file.

3. **"For Super Serious"**

Use this level of paper processing for:

- Purging piles of any size.

- Getting to the bottom of your stack.

- Prioritizing.

Label several boxes or trays according to these categories:

- Hot, Must Do or Things I Should Have Done Yesterday

- Warm, Should Do or Things I Can Put Off Until Tomorrow

- Cool, Nice To Do or Things I May Never Do

- To Read

- To Copy

"Genius is 99 percent perspiration and 1 percent inspiration."

—Thomas Edison

- To Refer

- To Delegate

- To File

- To Pay

- To Toss

Create any additional categories customized to your goals, work and personal activities.

TAKING CONTROL TIP #53

Clean your In box out every day, even if you haven't taken care of everything in it.

Something very important happens when you clean out your In box every day: you *prioritize* the items. You'll also be surprised at what you find in it. You see, one of the problems with In boxes is that they're convenient for tossing papers into—and many times you never look at them again.

At first, aim to have an empty In box at the end of each day. Then, as you get used to the idea of really using your In box rather than treating it as a convenient "catch-all," you'll find that you'll be cleaning it out a couple of times a day or as things pile up. You'll feel a great sense of accomplishment as you see the bottom of your In box on a regular basis.

Filing Tips for Finding Important Documents—Fast

A simple and easy-to-use filing system is a treasure. Depending on your situation, you may choose to file your "must-save" papers in one of these ways:

- Alphabetical, from A to Z (e.g., clients, products)

- Topical, by subject (e.g., sources, references, suppliers)

- Geographical, by location (e.g., sales territories, zip codes)

- Chronological, by date (e.g., minutes from board meetings)

- Numerical (e.g., invoices, job numbers)

Most people use a system that combines topical and alphabetical. This involves labeling a file folder by topic and then filing the individual folders alphabetically.

"A filing system is a place to lose things alphabetically."
—Author Unknown

SECTION • TWO

Overcoming Personal Disorganization

The following Taking Control Tips offer some general filing guidelines.

TAKING CONTROL TIP #54

Label your files clearly and descriptively.

"It's not how fast you can get it filed that counts, it's how fast you can find it."

—*Secretary Handbook,* Darnell Corporation, Chicago

- Label action files with verbs ("To Read," "To Pay").

- Label general files with nouns ("Mailing List," "Office Supplies," "Contract Negotiations," "Staff Meetings").

- Label hanging folders with a broad category and use individual files inside to be more specific ("Insurance" and then "Car Insurance," "Home Insurance," "Life Insurance").

- Color code when possible. Use a system of colored folders for separate projects and colored dots or labels for subcategories. Make the system easy to keep current and maintain.

CHAPTER • EIGHT

Who Says This Is a Paperless Society?

TAKING CONTROL TIP #55

Place the contents of a file so that when you open it, you can read it like a book. Place the most recent papers on top so the contents will be in chronological order and ready to read.

TAKING CONTROL TIP #56

Use a bright colored piece of heavy paper between sections of a single file folder to separate and subdivide information. It's easy to see clearly.

TAKING CONTROL TIP #57

As a general rule, never put more than three interior folders in a hanging file folder. If your files are very full, you will be less inclined to file or re-file your papers.

TAKING CONTROL TIP #58

To save time later, date every important letter you receive.

TAKING CONTROL TIP #59

Write the main subject or file name at the top right corner of the article.

The title of an article doesn't always reveal the topic. By writing the main subject of the article at the top, you avoid having to reread the article to see where to file it.

Who Says This Is a Paperless Society?

TAKING CONTROL TIP #60

Record the date of publication and the name of the magazine for any article you intend to file. That way, if you reference it later for any reason (e.g., in a report), you'll have the full citation at your fingertips.

Alternatives to Traditional File Cabinets

As stated previously, many people use a combination topical/alphabetical system for arranging files within a file cabinet. There are other places for keeping your important files, however.

SECTION • TWO

Overcoming Personal Disorganization

TAKING CONTROL TIP #61

Use a space near you (not in a file drawer!) for the files that help you most in your work.

For files you use often, consider using open plastic file boxes that hold six to twelve folders in a pending file arrangement. These boxes sit conveniently on your desk or credenza rather than being hidden inside a drawer.

TAKING CONTROL TIP #62

Use three-ring binders for keeping your notes on similar topics together.

Often, these binders are handier than individual files because within the binders you can further categorize your notes with tabbed divider pages. If you don't have enough room on your desktop or bookcase for binders, consider using the kind that hang in your file drawers.

Who Says This Is a Paperless Society?

TAKING CONTROL TIP #63

For items that you routinely refer to on the same day every month, use a tickler file.

This is a ready-made accordion folder with slots numbered from 1 to 31, corresponding to the days of the month. Place your documents in the numbered files that correspond to the date the documents need to be followed up on.

If you don't have enough papers crossing your desk to merit having a daily tickler, consider using a weekly or monthly tickler file. You can also create your own tickler with hanging files and file folders.

Maintaining Your Filing System

TAKING CONTROL TIP #64

Create a file weeding plan with a coding system that indicates how long to keep a file.

"Think before you file. Eighty percent of everything you file, you never look at again."

—Stephanie Culp, *Streamlining Your Life*

As you read files or papers you plan to file, quickly write the code in pencil on the top right corner of the front page. You'll have an easier time later when you're deciding whether or not to discard the item. Here's an example of an effective coding system:

M = Keep for this calendar month

Y = Keep for this calendar year

Y + 1 = Keep for this year and one more year

Y + 7 = Keep for this year and seven more years

P = Permanent; don't discard

UC = Keep until project or activity is complete

Who Says This Is a Paperless Society?

TAKING CONTROL TIP #65

Avoid "fat file-i-tis."

Be vigilant about file-weeding. Try one of these ideas:

- Weed one or two files around the one you just opened and worked on.

- Schedule five minutes a day for file-weeding. Set a timer so you don't get absorbed and wind up weeding for an hour.

TAKING CONTROL TIP #66

Beware of "file overkill."

It's easier to find and consult one file containing several pieces of paper than several files with only one item. For example, instead of keeping one file containing your five-year plan, another with the plan for the current year, and another with a list of personal goals, label one file "Planning" and keep all your planning documents in it. When it's time to plan, you'll need to consult all of these sheets anyway.

What to Do With All Those Articles You Say You're Going to Read

Getting the reading material you've accumulated under control is one of the more glorious benefits of getting organized. Obviously, reading is an important activity for keeping current with the constant changes occurring in your industry or field. Experts agree that in our fast-paced world, continuing to expand our knowledge is essential to success.

CHAPTER • EIGHT

Who Says This Is a Paperless Society?

TAKING CONTROL TIP #67

Create a portable "Read File."

Create a "Read File" out of a two-pocket folder.
Designate one pocket for articles you plan to
read and the other for articles you need to file.
Consider placing a highlighter, a pen and a small
pair of scissors in a small vinyl insert and keep it
with your "Read File." Carry the file with you for
browsing while you're waiting or when you have
a spare moment.

TAKING CONTROL TIP #68

Create a "To Read" box.

Create a place on your desk or in your work area for
a "To Read" box. Consider using a sturdy, horizontal
In box that has room to accommodate a hefty pile
of materials. Transfer the articles you consider to
be priority reading to your "Read File" (see Taking
Control Tip #67).

153

Organizing and Sorting Your Reading Material

When your reading material is really out of control, gather it all in stacks, or even boxes. Also have a pen, highlighter, stapler, scissors and trashbag handy.

Next, quickly go through your entire stack, placing things in piles. Make separate piles for magazines, articles and short reports, cartoons, ads and any other categories that fit your particular situation.

If you have personal and professional reading material mixed together, create separate categories for them.

TAKING CONTROL TIP #69

As you create your piles, throw out anything that's old, dated and useless or that you've decided is no longer worth your time to read.

You'll be amazed at how quickly your pile dwindles when you apply this tip.

TAKING CONTROL TIP #70

Prioritize each stack as you sort.

Or, if you prefer, prioritize as a separate step. The important thing is to prioritize so you'll know what to read first. If you don't prioritize, you'll waste time thumbing back through the stacks later.

Taking the Reading Plunge

Now that you have a handle on what and how much you have to read and the order in which you'll read it, consider one of these three methods for plunging in and actually reading it:

1. **The Easy-Does-It-Method.** Take fifteen minutes a day to sit in your favorite easy chair and relax and read. Set aside any articles you consider worth saving, and plan to file them later.

2. The Dead-Time Method. Place a few magazines or articles in your "Read File" and take it along with you to meetings or appointments. Use any dead time to your advantage. Transfer any articles you decide to save to the "To File" pocket. Throw away anything that isn't worth keeping.

3. The R and R and R Method. Take a well-stocked "Read File," or a whole box, to your favorite outdoor spot. Combine your rest and relaxation time with another "R"—Read.

TAKING CONTROL TIP #71

The key to committing yourself to reading the material you've saved is to schedule time to read it.

Even scheduling fifteen minutes a day translates to more than an hour during a regular five-day work week. You can get a lot of reading done in an hour.

Taking a Byte Out of Electronic Chaos

SECTION • TWO

Overcoming Personal Disorganization

"The illiterate of the future are those who cannot learn, unlearn or relearn."

—Alvin Toffler

Even if you're a low-tech person living in this high-tech age, you have to admit that computers have changed our lives with their lightning ability to store, organize, create and customize.

There's a computer program for just about anything you'd like to accomplish. That's why computers can be a real boost in TAKING CONTROL. A computer can also be a giant paperweight or a paper-making machine. It can save time, but it can also eat up time if you don't have the type of hardware and software you need to get the job done, if you don't keep your files organized, or if you develop poor working habits such as playing games or spending too much time tweaking your documents.

Taking a Byte Out of Electronic Chaos

Assessing Your Needs

TAKING CONTROL TIP #72

Before purchasing a computer, define what you need to accomplish.

The more specific you can be about the kinds of information you keep track of and how you need to manipulate it, the better you will know what computer equipment to purchase.

TAKING CONTROL TIP #73

Whether you use a computer or not, take a trip to a computer store and browse.

Ask questions. Pick up a catalog or computer magazine and browse through it. Even if you don't understand everything, you'll get a feel for how certain hardware and software can help you be even more productive.

Storing and Retrieving Computer Files

TAKING CONTROL TIP #74

Use a file name that clearly describes the file's content.

If you have a computer, you already know that it can be a wonderful way to store things, *if you can find them!* Clear file names that reflect what is actually in the file saves time and lessens stress. If the file name is clear, you won't have to open the file to see what's there. If you have to open the file to remember what's in it, then it's time to assign a new name.

TAKING CONTROL TIP #75

At least once a month, make a sweep through your directories and subdirectories to eliminate any files you no longer need.

Depending on the type of software you're using, you may be able to print a hard copy of your files organized by directory. This will make purging even easier—you can sort and clean up your directories. It'll be time well spent. Do this once a month and you'll be more organized.

TAKING CONTROL TIP #76

Back up your files according to a regular schedule.

There's nothing worse than spending several hours working to get a document "just right" and then losing it due to a system error or an electrical outage.

Every computer user knows the importance of backing up files. *Do it.* Regularly. Anyone who's lost files usually becomes a firm believer in backing up. Why wait until you lose something?

"To err is human, but to really foul things up requires a computer."
—Anonymous

More Important Tips for Using Your Computer to Take Control

TAKING CONTROL TIP #77

Take a computer class.

It doesn't matter how proficient you are, you will always benefit.

TAKING CONTROL TIP #78

Give yourself time to learn.

If you're just starting out on the road to computer literacy or learning a new software program, be patient with yourself as you learn. It'll be uphill for a while, but later you'll experience the productive side.

Handling E-mail

Electronic mail (e-mail) and memos have become substitutes for phone calls. Like the telephone, e-mail can become an interruption rather than a time-saving and convenient tool if you don't keep it under control.

TAKING CONTROL TIP #79

Develop a plan for handling the e-mail you receive.

Here are some suggestions:

- Check your e-mail several times a day. In fact, schedule time in your day for taking care of it.

- Don't let clutter collect in your e-mail mailbox. When you read it, buckle down and process your current messages all at one time. Do it, zap it, answer it, refer it, file it, print it, prioritize it or schedule time to work with a specific message. Think of your e-mail mailbox as another kind of In box and apply the same rules for keeping it under control.

"My rule always was to do the business of the day in the day."
—Duke of Wellington

TAKING CONTROL TIP #80

Don't contribute to e-mail clutter yourself.

Sometimes it's just too easy to send a message on e-mail, so people send and send and send some more. That results in e-mail clutter for your friends, colleagues and others. Here are some general guidelines for keeping e-mail simple:

- Keep each message to one topic.
- Keep your message brief, but do include all the details necessary for the recipient to properly respond.
- Clearly define the topic in the message header or subject line.
- Stifle the desire to send everyone you know a copy.

CHAPTER • NINE

Taking a Byte Out of Electronic Chaos

TAKING CONTROL TIP #81

If your e-mail system alerts you to
incoming mail with a beeping signal, turn
it off so that you're not interrupted by
every incoming message.

More Tips for Getting Organized and Energized

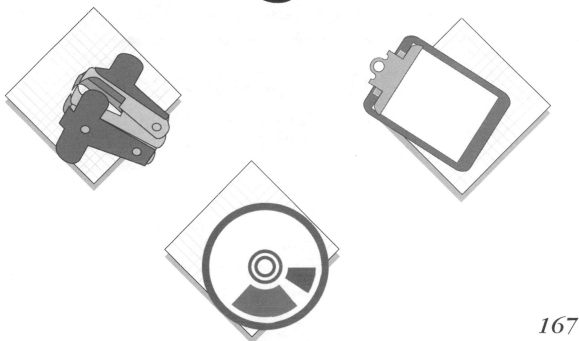

Little things can lighten your load …

TAKING CONTROL TIP #82

Shop once or twice a year for your greeting cards.

Keep a supply on hand for birthdays, anniversaries, sympathy, showers and so on. Create a file for each category. You can even save more time (and often, money) by ordering cards in bulk from direct mail greeting card catalogs.

TAKING CONTROL TIP #83

Keep a larger-than-you-think-you'll-ever-need supply of stamps on hand.

Save time by ordering stamps by phone: 1-800-STAMP-24. Call day or night. The post office knows about people who are trying to get organized!

More Tips for Getting Organized and Energized

TAKING CONTROL TIP #84

Learn how to speed read.

Train yourself or take a course. Or, if speed reading isn't something that interests you, skim an article, book or report for general ideas to see if you care about reading the specifics.

TAKING CONTROL TIP #85

Enroll in "Audio University."

Listen to audio programs in your car. Enrich yourself personally and professionally. Become a "road" scholar as you roll along.

TAKING CONTROL TIP #86

To avoid interruptions, create busy signs for each occasion. People will notice them more. Even if your cubicle has no "door," consider posting a sign that says "Door Closed" once in awhile. Take the sign down immediately after your DO NOT DISTURB time.

TAKING CONTROL TIP #87

Consider hiring a professional organizer.

When you know you need a pro:

- Your mother is coming to live with you
- You have to prepare your house for sale
- You're getting married or divorced
- You're having a baby
- You're going back to school

More Tips for Getting Organized and Energized

- You're redecorating or adding on to your home

- Your home-based business is growing and creating chaos

- You know you'd use a system but you need someone to teach you one

- You want something organized f-a-s-t!

- You have a panic attack just thinking about organizing all by yourself

There's no shame in yelling "Help!" A professional organizer can help you set up a system specifically for your needs and lifestyle and teach you to use it. Contact the National Association of Professional Organizers (NAPO) for a list of pros in your area:

National Association of Professional Organizers
15000 Commerce Parkway
Suite C
Mount Laurel, NJ 08054
Phone: (856) 380-6828
Fax: (856) 439-0525

Most people don't even know there is such an organization!

"It's amazing what ordinary people can do if they set out without preconceived notions."
—Charles Kettering

TAKING CONTROL TIP #88

Don't underestimate the power of address labels or an address stamp.

They can save you incredible amounts of time and effort. Order them!

TAKING CONTROL TIP #89

Create project briefcases.

"Do what you can, with what you have, where you are."

—Theodore Roosevelt

Assign one hobby or project per briefcase—secondhand ones do nicely. Keep everything on a certain subject in one case, ready to grab when you need it.

CHAPTER · TEN

More Tips for Getting Organized and Energized

TAKING CONTROL TIP #90

Know your own energy peaks and valleys. Daily fluctuations in physical and emotional energy affects productivity. Schedule critical activities for your prime time.

TAKING CONTROL TIP #91

Be realistic about how long things take to do. Most people underestimate by a factor of two to four how much time a given task will require.

TAKING CONTROL TIP #92

Create checklists for repetitive jobs.

For grocery shopping, packing for business travel, replenishing office supplies and other routine tasks that usually require making a list, do the thinking *once* by creating a comprehensive checklist. Make copies of these lists, and each time you need to perform the task, check off the items you need from the appropriate lists.

TAKING CONTROL TIP #93

Create a job jar.

"And now the matchless deed's achiev'd, Determined, dared, and done."

—Christopher Smart

As the "when-I-can-get-around-to them" tasks occur to you, write them on slips of paper and place them in the jar. Write "job jar" on your calendar in a given time slot, at regular intervals. When that day and time comes, pull a job out and work on it! (You can always exchange it for another job if you don't like the one you pulled, but at least you're getting something done!) Use the job jar idea to get your family or staff involved.

More Tips for Getting Organized and Energized

TAKING CONTROL TIP #94

Save time by doing things when others aren't.

Consider how much time you waste waiting in long lines and fighting crowds. Here are some ideas for avoiding some common crowd-crushing scenes:

- Don't cash checks on Friday afternoons.

- Go grocery shopping during the dinner hour or after 9 p.m.

- Go to restaurants early, before the dinner crowd.

- Use the office photocopier during lunch when everyone else is gone.

"Read every day something no one else is reading. Think every day something no one else is thinking. It is bad for the mind to be always part of unanimity."

—Christopher Morley

Office Supplies for the Well-Equipped Office

Decide the items you'll need for your work. Keep what you need at hand and the rest in the supply closet or cabinet.

TAKING CONTROL TIP #95

Create an inventory list and post a copy in the supply area so you can easily check off items that need replenishing.

Here is a sample of some of the items you'll find in any well-stocked office. Use it as a starting point for developing your own list.

- Automatic pencil sharpener
- Bulletin board
- Calculator
- Cellophane tape
- Computer printer supplies (paper, toner)
- Computer supplies (CD-ROMs, etc.)
- Envelopes, letter and manila

More Tips for Getting Organized and Energized

- File folders
- Flip chart and stand
- Glue stick
- Hanging files
- Hole punch
- Labels for file folders
- Legal pads
- Letter opener
- Mailing labels
- Markers
- Message pads
- Note pads
- Paper
- Paper clips
- Pencils and pens
- Phone book
- Photocopier supplies (paper, toner)
- Postal scale
- Push pins
- Ring binders
- Ruler
- Scissors

"Time is not a line, but a series of now-points."
—Taisen
   Deshimaru

SECTION • TWO

Overcoming Personal Disorganization

- Stamps
- Stapler
- Stationery
- Sticky notes
- White board

What to Do Now That You're So Organized

- Smile… then grin!

- Watch a sunset.

- Listen to your favorite music with your eyes closed.

- Look out the window and watch the world hurry by.

- Call up a friend and chat.

- Write in your journal.

- Start a journal.

- Plan that dream trip.

- Eat your favorite treat … slowly.

"There must be a beginning of any great matter, but the continuing unto the end until it be thouroughly finished yields the true glory."
—Sir Francis Drake

Bibliography and Suggested Reading

Aslett, Don. *Not For Packrats Only: How to Clean Up, Clear Out, and Live Clutter-Free Forever.* New York: Plume, 1991.

Covey, Stephen R. *The Seven Habits of Highly Effective People: Restoring the Character Ethic.* New York: Simon and Schuster, 1990.

Culp, Stephanie. *Streamlining Your Life: A 5-Point Plan for Uncomplicated Living.* Cincinnati, OH: Writer's Digest Books, 1991.

Dorff, Pat. *File... Don't Pile: For People Who Write: Handling the Paper Flow in the Workspace or Home Office.* New York: St. Martin's, 1994.

Gleeson, Kerry. *The Personal Efficiency Program (PEP).* New York: Wiley, 1994.

Lakein, Alan. *How to Get Control of Your Time and Your Life.* New York: Signet, 1974.

Pollar, Odette. *Organizing Your Work Space.* Menlo Park: Crisp Publications, 1992.

BIBLIOGRAPHY

and Suggested Reading

Silver, Susan. *Organized to Be the Best! Winning Solutions to Simplify How You Work.* Los Angeles, CA: Adams-Hall, 1989.

Temme, Jim. *Productivity Power: 250 Great Ideas for Being More Productive.* Mission, KS: SkillPath Publications, 1993.

Winston, Stephanie. *The Organized Executive: New Ways to Manage Time, Paper, People, and the Electronic Office.* New York: W.W. Norton, 1994.

Index: Ending With the Beginning in Mind

"Someone once told me that time was a predator stalking you your whole life. I rather think it's a companion following you through the journey, reminding you to cherish every moment, because it'll never come again."

—Captain Jean Luc Picard, Starship Enterprise, in the movie *Star Trek: Generations*

INDEX

INDEX

Ending With the Beginning in Mind

"What you can do, or dream you can do, begin it. Boldness has genius, power and magic in it. Only engage, and then the mind grows heated—Begin it, and the work will be completed!"

—Goethe

INDEX

Ending With the Beginning in Mind

Available From SkillPath Publications

Self-Study Sourcebooks

Climbing the Corporate Ladder: What You Need to Know and Do to Be a Promotable Person by Barbara Pachter and Marjorie Brody

Coping With Supervisory Nightmares: 12 Common Nightmares of Leadership and What You Can Do About Them by Michael and Deborah Singer Dobson

Defeating Procrastination: 52 Fail-Safe Tips for Keeping Time on Your Side by Marlene Caroselli, Ed.D.

Discovering Your Purpose by Ivy Haley

Going for the Gold: Winning the Gold Medal for Financial Independence by Lesley D. Bissett, CFP

Having Something to Say When You Have to Say Something: The Art of Organizing Your Presentation by Randy Horn

Info-Flood: How to Swim in a Sea of Information Without Going Under by Marlene Caroselli, Ed.D.

The Innovative Secretary by Marlene Caroselli, Ed.D.

Letters & Memos: Just Like That! by Dave Davies

Mastering the Art of Communication: Your Keys to Developing a More Effective Personal Style by Michelle Fairfield Poley

Organized for Success! 95 Tips for Taking Control of Your Time, Your Space, and Your Life by Nanci McGraw

A Passion to Lead! How to Develop Your Natural Leadership Ability by Michael Plumstead

P.E.R.S.U.A.D.E.: Communication Strategies That Move People to Action by Marlene Caroselli, Ed.D.

Productivity Power: 250 Great Ideas for Being More Productive by Jim Temme

Promoting Yourself: 50 Ways to Increase Your Prestige, Power, and Paycheck by Marlene Caroselli, Ed.D.

Risk-Taking: 50 Ways to Turn Risks Into Rewards by Marlene Caroselli, Ed.D. and David Harris

Speak Up and Stand Out: How to Make Effective Presentations by Nanci McGraw

Stress Control: How You Can Find Relief From Life's Daily Stress by Steve Bell

The Technical Writer's Guide by Robert McGraw

Total Quality Customer Service: How to Make It Your Way of Life by Jim Temme

Write It Right! A Guide for Clear and Correct Writing by Richard Andersen and Helene Hinis

Your Total Communication Image by Janet Signe Olson, Ph.D.

Handbooks

The ABC's of Empowered Teams: Building Blocks for Success by Mark Towers

Assert Yourself! Developing Power-Packed Communication Skills to Make Your Points Clearly, Confidently, and Persuasively by Lisa Contini

Breaking the Ice: How to Improve Your On-the-Spot Communication Skills
by Deborah Shouse

The Care and Keeping of Customers: A Treasury of Facts, Tips and Proven Techniques for Keeping Your Customers Coming BACK! by Roy Lantz

Challenging Change: Five Steps for Dealing With Change by Holly DeForest and Mary Steinberg

Dynamic Delegation: A Manager's Guide for Active Empowerment by Mark Towers

Every Woman's Guide to Career Success by Denise M. Dudley

Hiring and Firing: What Every Manager Needs to Know by Marlene Caroselli, Ed.D. with Laura Wyeth, Ms.Ed.

How to Be a More Effective Group Communicator: How to Find Your Role and Boost Your Confidence in Group Situations by Deborah Shouse

How to Deal With Difficult People by Paul Friedman

Learning to Laugh at Work: The Power of Humor in the Workplace by Robert McGraw

Making Your Mark: How to Develop a Personal Marketing Plan for Becoming More Visible and More Appreciated at Work by Deborah Shouse

Meetings That Work by Marlene Caroselli, Ed.D.

The Mentoring Advantage: How to Help Your Career Soar to New Heights by Pam Grout

Minding Your Business Manners: Etiquette Tips for Presenting Yourself Professionally in Every Business Situation by Marjorie Brody and Barbara Pachter

Misspeller's Guide by Joel and Ruth Schroeder

Motivation in the Workplace: How to Motivate Workers to Peak Performance and Productivity by Barbara Fielder

NameTags Plus: Games You Can Play When People Don't Know What to Say by Deborah Shouse

Networking: How to Creatively Tap Your People Resources by Colleen Clarke

New & Improved! 25 Ways to Be More Creative and More Effective by Pam Grout

Power Write! A Practical Guide to Words That Work by Helene Hinis

The Power of Positivity: Eighty Ways to Energize Your Life by Joel and Ruth Schroeder

Putting Anger to Work For You! by Ruth and Joel Schroeder

Reinventing Your Self: 28 Strategies for Coping With Change by Mark Towers

Saying "No" to Negativity: How to Manage Negativity in Yourself, Your Boss and Your Co-Workers by Zoie Kaye

The Supervisor's Guide: The Everyday Guide to Coordinating People and Tasks by Jerry Brown and Denise Dudley, Ph.D.

Taking Charge: A Personal Guide to Managing Projects and Priorities by Michal E. Feder

Treasure Hunt: 10 Stepping Stones to a New and More Confident You! by Pam Grout

A Winning Attitude: How to Develop Your Most Important Asset! by Michelle Fairfield Poley

For more information, call 1-800-873-7545.